A TASTE OF STAR WARS

SNACKS

A TASTE OF

SNACKS

Bite-Size Recipes
in a Snack-Size Book

SAN RAFAEL · LOS ANGELES · LONDON

CONTENTS

7 Introduction

SAVORY

9 Omega's Popcorn Mix
13 Grogu's Avocado Dip
17 Jawa Sushi
21 Bright Tree Village Salad
25 Ylesian White Worms
29 Constable's Caps
33 Maul Pancakes
36 Mon Cala Sardine Fritters
41 Chopper Cheese Toast
45 Rings of Hudalla
49 Pickled Paddy Flowers
53 Spiced Bogwings

SWEET

- 57 Loth-Cat Kibble
- 61 Butter Chewies
- 65 Fruit TIE Fighters
- 69 Ahsoka's Jelly Cubes
- 73 Dagobah Swamp Vines
- 77 Won-Taun Tundra Treats
- 81 Wookiee-Ookiees
- 85 Bespin Cloud Drops
- 89 Mustafarian Lava Buns
- 93 BB-8 Cupcakes
- 97 Kyber Scones
- 101 Klatooine Crêpes
- 105 TIE Fighter Ice Cream Sandwiches
- 109 Pasaana Pops

DIETARY KEY
V: Vegetarian
V*: Easily Made Vegetarian
V+: Vegan
V+*: Easily Made Vegan
GF: Gluten Free
GF*: Easily Made Gluten Free

INTRODUCTION

Welcome to *A Taste of Star Wars: Snacks*, a bite-size cookbook filled with savory and sweet recipes inspired by the *Star Wars* galaxy.

Whether you're honoring your favorite heroes with Ahsoka's Jelly Cubes and Grogu's Avocado Dip or taking a bite out of the dark side with Maul Pancakes and Fruit TIE Fighters, dig into this scrumptious selection of snacks—including vegetarian, vegan, and gluten-free options—to celebrate your love of all things *Star Wars*.

Enjoy, and may the Force be with you!

OMEGA'S POPCORN MIX

Omega and Wrecker of the Bad Batch love to celebrate a successful mission with a bag of Mantell Mix, a snack from the planet Ord Mantell. Inspired by Omega's favorite snack, this sweet and savory popcorn mix is a great way to treat yourself for your own successes.

OMEGA'S POPCORN MIX

Prep Time: 15 minutes | **Cook Time:** 5 minutes
V*, GF* | **Yield:** 8 servings
Difficulty: Easy

8 cups freshly popped popcorn, divided
4 ounces purple chocolate candy melts
2 tablespoons unsalted butter, melted
2 teaspoons granulated sugar
½ teaspoon cinnamon
¼ teaspoon kosher salt
¼ cup dried raspberries
¼ cup shelled pistachios

1. Prep a baking sheet by lining it with parchment paper. Set aside.
2. Divide the popcorn in half, into two large bowls.

3. In a microwave-safe bowl, melt the chocolate candy melts for 30 seconds and then stir.

4. Heat again for two 15-second intervals, stirring in between until melted and smooth. Toss with one of the bowls of popcorn and then spread the candy-coated popcorn onto one side of the prepped baking sheet.

5. Toss the second bowl of popcorn with the butter, sugar, cinnamon, and salt. Spread onto the other side of the baking sheet.

6. When the candy melts have set, toss the two popcorn mixes together along with the dried raspberries and pistachios. Serve.

NOTE: Use vegetarian gluten-free candy melts to make this gluten free and vegetarian.

GROGU'S AVOCADO DIP

Grogu loves nothing more than something yummy to munch on, and with this rich and creamy avocado dip, you'll have a snack that the little foundling himself would approve of.

GROGU'S AVOCADO DIP

Prep Time: 15 minutes
V, GF* | Yield: 2 servings
Difficulty: Medium

2 medium avocados, peeled and pitted
½ cup plain fat-free Greek yogurt
¼ cup cilantro, stemmed
1 garlic clove, peeled
1 tablespoon minced shallot
1 tablespoon lime juice
½ teaspoon kosher salt
¼ teaspoon onion powder
¼ teaspoon white pepper
2 kalamata olives
2 slices pink apples
2 pitas, for serving

1. Into the base of a blender add the avocados, Greek yogurt, cilantro, garlic, shallot, lime juice, salt, onion powder, and white pepper. Blend until just combined.
2. To create Grogu's head, spread the sauce into an oval shape. Add a curved triangle on both sides to make the ears. Then add a small dollop of sauce for the nose.
3. Add the kalamata olives to create the eyes and add the pink apple for the ears. Use the back of a knife's blade to create his eyebrows by drawing one horizontal line above each of the kalamata olives. Draw four vertical lines in between the two horizontal lines, to finish off the face details.
4. Cut the edges off one pita to create a long trapezoid. Place this under the head to create the robe. Cut the other pita into four smaller pieces to create the overlapping scarf and the cuffs. Add a small spoonful of the sauce on top of the cuffs to create the hands.
5. Serve the sauce with the remaining pita.

NOTE: This is easily made gluten free by using a gluten-free pita option.

JAWA SUSHI

If you see a Jawa get excited, you might hear them say "Utinni!" With a plate of these yummy, Jawa-shaped sushi pockets, you might end up saying "Utinni!" yourself.

JAWA SUSHI

Prep Time: 30 minutes | **Cook Time:** 20 minutes
V, GF | **Yield:** 10 pieces
Difficulty: Medium

RICE:
1 cup short grain brown rice
1½ cups water
1½ tablespoons rice vinegar
1 tablespoon granulated sugar
¼ teaspoon kosher salt

GARNISH:
1 large egg
1 tablespoon olive oil
10 seasoned tofu pouches
1 sheet nori, cut into 3-by-3-inch squares

1. **TO MAKE THE RICE:** Rinse the rice until water runs clear. Soak in cold water for 25 minutes and then drain.

2. In a large pot, add the rice and water. Bring to a boil. Cover and reduce heat and then simmer for 20 minutes until the water is absorbed. Remove from heat and let sit for 10 minutes, covered.

3. Transfer the rice into a large bowl and fold in the rice vinegar, sugar, and salt. Let cool slightly.

4. **TO MAKE THE GARNISH:** In a small bowl, use a fork to scramble the egg. In a small pan over medium heat, add the oil and pour in the egg. When the bottom has set, fold the edges over to form an omelet. Remove from pan and set aside.

5. Carefully pull open the tofu pouch. Stuff with 3 to 4 tablespoons of rice. Place a piece of nori on the outside.

6. Use a tiny round cutter to cut out circles from the omelet and then place on the nori to form the eyes. Repeat with the remaining tofu pouches and rice.

BRIGHT TREE VILLAGE SALAD

The forest moon of Endor is like a planet-size pantry, covered in all sorts of veggies, berries, nuts, and other edible plants. This colorful salad, made from thinly sliced carrots and daikon radish, could be enjoyed by the Ewoks of Bright Tree Village as a light and refreshing bite before a big feast.

BRIGHT TREE VILLAGE SALAD

Prep Time: 5 minutes
V, V+, GF* | Yield: 6 servings
Difficulty: Easy

2 tablespoons rice vinegar
1 tablespoon granulated sugar
1 teaspoon mirin
½ teaspoon sesame oil
2 cups daikon radish, julienned
1 cup carrots, julienned
1 teaspoon black sesame seeds

1. In a large bowl, whisk the rice vinegar, sugar, mirin, and sesame oil. Stir until the sugar has dissolved.
2. Toss the radish and carrots with the vinegar mixture. Top with sesame seeds, to serve.

NOTE: Use a gluten-free mirin to ensure this is gluten free.

YLESIAN WHITE WORMS

The Hutt gangsters of the Outer Rim enjoy many unusual delicacies, but one of their favorites is the white worm larvae from the planet Ylesia. If that doesn't sound appealing, try these seasoned balls of semi-soft cheese instead. Their taste and consistency could fool Jabba himself, with all of the spice and none of the squirm!

YLESIAN WHITE WORMS

Prep Time: 10 minutes
V, GF | Yield: 4 servings
Difficulty: Easy

½ cup extra-virgin olive oil
4 garlic cloves, peeled and rough chopped
1 tablespoon fresh chopped basil
1 teaspoon oregano
1 teaspoon parsley
¼ teaspoon dried red pepper flakes
¼ teaspoon sweet smoked paprika
¼ teaspoon lemon pepper
¼ teaspoon kosher salt
8 ounces fresh mozzarella balls, drained

1. In a small bowl, stir together the olive oil, garlic, basil, oregano, parsley, pepper flakes, paprika, lemon pepper, and salt.
2. Toss the mozzarella balls with the oil mixture.
3. Place into an airtight container and refrigerate for 2 to 4 hours, until ready to serve.

CONSTABLE'S CAPS

These savory stuffed mushrooms are named for their resemblance to the iconic disk-shaped helmets worn by Constable Zuvio and the other Kyuzo enforcers who patrol Jakku's Niima Outpost. It's the perfect homage, because taste this spectacular can't possibly be legal!

CONSTABLE'S CAPS

Prep Time: 10 minutes | **Cook Time:** 15 minutes
V | Yield: Servings vary
Difficulty: Medium

1 pound button mushrooms
3 tablespoons unsalted butter
1 clove garlic, minced
½ cup panko breadcrumbs
¼ cup grated Parmesan cheese
2 green onions, both white and green parts, finely chopped
1 tablespoon finely chopped parsley
½ teaspoon garam masala
Kosher salt
Freshly ground black pepper

1. Preheat the oven to 350°F and line a baking sheet with parchment paper or a silicone mat.

2. Clean and stem the mushrooms and dice the stems small. Arrange the mushroom caps on the baking sheet, leaving a little room between each.

3. Melt the butter in a medium sauté pan or skillet over medium heat. Add the garlic and cook for 2 to 3 minutes, until soft and fragrant. Add the diced mushroom stems and cook for about 5 minutes, until they have released their juices.

4. Stir in the breadcrumbs, Parmesan cheese, green onions, parsley, garam masala, and salt and pepper to taste, and cook 1 minute more, until the cheese is softened and everything is incorporated. Remove from the heat.

5. Using a small spoon, press the filling into the hollows of the mushroom caps. Continue adding filling, mounding it up on top of each cap. Bake for about 15 minutes, until the mushrooms are soft. Serve hot.

MAUL PANCAKES

There's no doubt that Darth Maul is one of the most fearsome warriors in the galaxy. This pancake mimics the Sith Lord's scowling visage and is filled with kimchi, which gives it a fiery hue worthy of Maul's raging temperament.

MAUL PANCAKES

Prep Time: 10 minutes | **Cook Time:** 10 minutes
V, V+, GF* | **Yield:** 1 pancake
Difficulty: Medium

½ cup all-purpose flour
½ cup mochiko
½ cup soy milk
1 tablespoon gochujang
1 cup chopped kimchi
1 green onion, minced
1 tablespoon vegetable oil
3 to 4 tablespoons black sesame seeds
1 small white onion
½ teaspoon sriracha hot sauce

1. In a large bowl, whisk together the flour and mochiko. Make a well in the center and stir in the soy milk and gochujang. Fold in the kimchi and green onions.

2. In a large skillet over medium heat, add oil and pour the batter into the pan, spreading to flatten into a large pancake.

3. Cook for 3 to 4 minutes, until lightly browned. Flip over and cook for another 2 to 3 minutes, until cooked through.

4. Move the pancake to a serving plate. Use the black sesame seeds to create Maul's face pattern.

5. Slice the onions to create his horns, eyes, and teeth. Add the sriracha and 2 black sesame seeds for the pupils. Serve immediately.

NOTE: To make this recipe gluten free, use gluten-free all-purpose flour and check your gochujang and kimchi to make sure they're gluten free.

MON CALA SARDINE FRITTERS

This salty fish cake draws inspiration from the aquatic world of Mon Cala. In fact, its fantastic flavors would probably be one of the few things that a couple of the planet's native species, the Mon Calamari and the Quarren, could actually agree on!

MON CALA SARDINE FRITTERS

Prep Time: 5 minutes | **Cook Time:** 15 minutes
Yield: About 20 fritters
Difficulty: Easy

Oil for frying, such as canola
Two 5-ounce tins sardines, drained
1 egg
6 pieces seaweed snack, flaked small
Squeeze of fresh lime juice
1 tablespoon sesame seeds
Pinch of cayenne pepper
½ cup panko breadcrumbs
Kosher salt
Freshly ground black pepper

1. Using two forks, mash the sardines to a paste in a medium bowl.
2. Add the egg, seaweed, lime juice, sesame seeds, and cayenne, and season with salt and pepper to taste.
3. Add the breadcrumbs until you have a mixture that is neither too wet nor too dry but can be shaped easily by hand. Form into balls about 1 inch across.
4. Fill a small saucepan with about 1 inch of oil and place over medium heat.

5. Working in batches, add the fritters to the hot oil, making sure not to overcrowd them. Turn the fritters occasionally until they are a dark golden brown on all sides, about 5 minutes total.

6. Remove to a plate lined with paper towels and repeat until all the fritters are cooked.

CHOPPER CHEESE TOAST

Now this is the droid you're looking for! These grilled cheese sandwiches are stacked to look like Chopper, the loyal (but cranky) droid who is never too far from the rebel hero Hera Syndulla.

CHOPPER CHEESE TOAST

Prep Time: 15 minutes | **Cook Time:** 2 minutes
Yield: 2 toasts
Difficulty: Medium

2 slices white bread
2 slices white cheddar cheese
2 slices American cheese
1 slice ham

1. Cut the crusts off one piece of bread, creating a 5-by-5-inch square. Place onto a quarter baking sheet lined with parchment paper. Place a piece of white cheddar on top. Set aside.

2. Cut the second slice of bread into a trapezoid with a 5-inch base and that is 3 inches tall. Position this above the square piece of bread. Cut a piece of American cheese to fit and place on the trapezoid.

3. Use the bread scraps to create Chopper's legs. These should look like an "L."
4. Cut pieces of cheese and ham to create Chopper's details.
5. Place the baking sheet into a toaster oven and lightly toast for 1 to 2 minutes until the cheese has melted.

RINGS OF HUDALLA

The planet Hudalla is an enormous gas giant orbited by some of the largest rings in the galaxy. It's impressive to behold—but not nearly as impressive as these scrumptious bacon-wrapped onion rings that share its name!

RINGS OF HUDALLA

Prep Time: 15 minutes | **Cook Time:** 30 minutes
GF | **Yield:** Servings vary
Difficulty: Medium

2 large yellow onions, peeled and cut into ½-inch-thick disks
2 tablespoons hot sauce
1 cup packed brown sugar
½ teaspoon garam masala
1 pound sliced bacon

1. Preheat the oven to 400°F. Line a baking sheet with aluminum foil to catch any drips and set a cooling rack on top.

2. Divide the sliced onions into sections of two same-size rings sandwiched together, which will give some stability as they bake. Choose the largest rings and work smaller from there. Lightly brush each pair of rings with hot sauce.

3. In a small bowl, combine the brown sugar and garam masala, then dip each slice of bacon in the sugar mix.

4. Wrap each onion in one or more slices of sugary bacon, making sure the bacon doesn't overlap and covers most of the onion. Place each wrapped ring on the cooling rack over the prepared baking sheet.

5. Bake for about 30 minutes, until the bacon is crisp but the rings hold their shape. If you'd like the bacon any crisper, slide the baking sheet under the broiler very briefly. Enjoy while still warm but be careful—they will be hot from the oven.

PICKLED PADDY FLOWERS

The slug-like gangsters known as the Hutts have been known to crave the taste of Klatooine paddy frogs. For those who prefer a snack that's a bit less lively, these brined cucumbers manage to capture similarly salty flavors—with significantly less wriggling as they slide down your throat!

PICKLED PADDY FLOWERS

Prep Time: 15 minutes
V, V+, GF | Yield: 4 servings
Difficulty: Easy

2 cups peeled and sliced English cucumber
½ teaspoon kosher salt
3 tablespoons granulated sugar
2 tablespoons white vinegar

1. Toss the cucumber and salt and place in a colander to drain for 15 minutes.
2. In a large bowl toss the cucumber, sugar, and vinegar. Toss to coat and refrigerate until ready to serve.

SPICED BOGWINGS

Bogwings are reptavian creatures that are native to Naboo, and their meat is sold at markets across the Outer Rim. These spicy, saucy chicken wings are the perfect tribute to that mouthwatering snack!

SPICED BOGWINGS

Prep Time: 10 minutes | **Cook Time:** 50 minutes
GF* | **Yield:** 15 to 20 wings
Difficulty: Medium

CHICKEN:
3 pounds chicken wings
1½ tablespoons baking powder
1 teaspoon garlic powder
1 teaspoon onion powder
¼ teaspoon kosher salt
¼ teaspoon freshly ground black pepper

SAUCE:
¼ cup soy sauce
2 tablespoons packed light brown sugar
1 tablespoon gochujang
1 tablespoon rice vinegar
2 teaspoons gochugaru (Korean red pepper flakes)
1 teaspoon sesame oil
2 garlic cloves, minced

1. Preheat the oven to 400°F. Place a wire rack on a baking sheet.
2. **TO MAKE THE CHICKEN:** In a large bowl, toss the chicken wings with the baking powder, garlic powder, onion powder, salt, and black pepper. Place the seasoned wings on the prepped wire rack.
3. Bake the wings for 30 minutes, flip them, then bake for another 20 minutes, until the wings are golden brown.
4. **TO MAKE THE SAUCE:** While the wings cook, in a large bowl, stir together the soy sauce, brown sugar, gochujang, vinegar, gochugaru, sesame oil, and garlic.
5. When the wings are done, add them to the sauce and toss until coated.
6. Turn the oven to broil. Place the wings back on the wire rack and broil for 1 minute, until crispy. Serve hot.

NOTE: This is easily made gluten free by using gluten-free soy sauce and gochujang.

LOTH-CAT KIBBLE

Inspired by the Loth-cats found on the grassy plains of Lothal, this crunchy kibble was created specifically for humans. Crunchy, sweet, and salty, this tasty snack will satisfy most cravings.

LOTH-CAT KIBBLE

Prep Time: 30 minutes
V, GF* | Yield: About 8 cups
Difficulty: Easy

1 cup peanut butter chips, divided
½ cup milk chocolate chips
4 tablespoons unsalted butter
1 teaspoon kosher salt
½ cup smooth natural peanut butter
4 cups peanut butter–flavor crunchy corn and oat cereal
4 cups regular crunchy corn and oat cereal
2 cups powdered sugar

1. Mix ½ cup peanut butter chips, the milk chocolate chips, butter, and salt together in a microwave-safe bowl. Heat mixture in microwave on 50 percent power, stirring once or twice, until chips are melted and butter is fully incorporated, about 3 minutes. Remove from microwave and stir in peanut butter.

2. Place both cereals in a very large bowl and pour chocolate mixture over. Gently stir to coat all the cereal. Once coated, add powdered sugar and gently stir again to fully coat all the cereal. Spread out onto a large-rimmed baking sheet to cool completely.

3. Once cooled, add remaining peanut butter chips and stir to combine.

4. Store at room temperature in an airtight container.

NOTE: This can be made gluten free by using gluten-free cereal options.

BUTTER CHEWIES

Chewbacca likes to think with his stomach, and sometimes it lands him and Han Solo in trouble. But can you blame him? We're all a little food-motivated, at times. When was the last time you treated yourself with a special snack after a tiring day? Next time, try preparing a plate of coconut-topped butter mochi. These mini versions of Chewie are nutty, rich, and, well . . . chewy!

BUTTER CHEWIES

Prep Time: 20 minutes | **Cook Time:** 1 hour
V*, GF* | **Yield:** 12 bars
Difficulty: Medium

MOCHI:
16 ounces mochiko
2½ cups granulated sugar
1½ teaspoons baking powder
¼ teaspoon kosher salt
One 14-ounce can coconut milk
One 12-ounce can evaporated milk
½ cup (1 stick) unsalted butter, melted
4 large eggs, beaten slightly
2 teaspoons vanilla extract

TOPPING:
1½ cups shredded coconut
2 tablespoons granulated sugar
½ teaspoon cinnamon

DECORATION:
4 ounces chocolate candy melts
2 ounces black candy melts
2 ounces white candy melts

1. Preheat the oven to 350°F. Prep a 13-by-9-inch pan with parchment paper and nonstick spray.

2. **TO MAKE THE MOCHI:** In a large bowl whisk together the mochiko, sugar, baking powder, and salt. Make a well in the center of the dry ingredients and stir in the coconut milk, evaporated milk, butter, eggs, and vanilla. Pour into the prepped pan.

3. **TO MAKE THE TOPPING:** In a small bowl mix together the coconut, sugar, and cinnamon. Sprinkle over the batter. Bake for 1 hour, until set.

4. Let cool completely. Use a plastic knife to cut into 12 rectangles.

5. In a microwave-safe bowl, melt the chocolate candy melts for 30 seconds, then stir. Heat again for two 15-second intervals, stirring in between until melted and smooth. Pour into a piping bag. Set aside. Do the same for the black and white candy melts.

6. **TO DECORATE:** Use the chocolate candy melts to pipe a bandolier in a diagonal across the mochi. Then pipe the black icing to create the Wookiee's eyes and nose.

7. Finally, use the candy melts to create the teeth and bandolier details.

8. Once the candy melts have set, the mochi is ready to serve.

> **NOTE:** Use vegetarian gluten-free candy melts to make this gluten free and vegetarian.

FRUIT TIE FIGHTERS

TIE fighters are fearsome ships employed by both the Galactic Empire and the dastardly First Order. TIEs often swarm their enemies with powerful cannons and swift speed. Thanks to some tangy apples, this fruity treat packs a similar punch.

FRUIT TIE FIGHTERS

Prep Time: 15 minutes
V, V+, GF | Yield: 6 TIE fighters
Difficulty: Easy

2 large Granny Smith green apples
2 kiwis

SPECIAL TOOLS:
6 toothpicks

1. Slice and cut the apples into twelve hexagon shapes. Set aside.

2. Peel the kiwi and slice into six ½-inch-thick rounds. Poke a toothpick lengthwise through the kiwi round. Skewer a slice of apple onto both ends, so the TIE fighter stands up by itself. Repeat with the remaining apples and kiwi to form six TIE fighters.

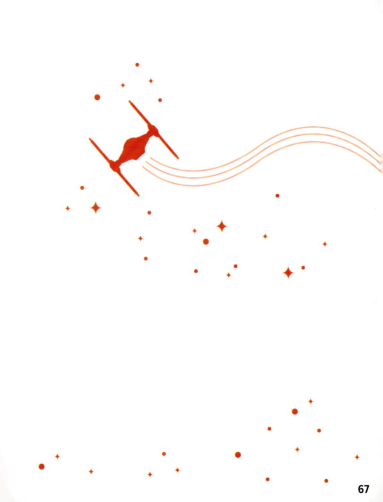

67

AHSOKA'S JELLY CUBES

Once the Padawan of Anakin Skywalker, Ahsoka Tano leaves the Jedi Order to find her own path, eventually serving as one of the founding members of the Rebel Alliance. The bright blue, orange, and white colors of this sweet jelly are a stunning homage to Ahsoka Tano, one of the bravest, most independent heroes that the galaxy has ever seen.

AHSOKA'S JELLY CUBES

Prep Time: 24 hours
GF | Yield: 12 cubes
Difficulty: Medium

ORANGE GELATIN:
6 ounces orange gelatin
2 cups boiling water

BLUE GELATIN:
6 ounces blue raspberry gelatin
2 cups boiling water

WHITE GELATIN:
2 envelopes unflavored gelatin
2 cups boiling water
One 14-ounce can sweetened condensed milk

1. **TO MAKE THE ORANGE GELATIN:** In a medium bowl, dissolve the orange gelatin into the boiling water. Whisk until clear. Pour into a small container, and cover. Set aside.

2. **TO MAKE THE BLUE GELATIN:** In a separate medium bowl, dissolve the blue raspberry gelatin into the boiling water. Whisk until clear. Pour into a separate small container, and cover.

3. Refrigerate both gelatins for 5 hours or until solid.

4. When solid, cut gelatin into cubes and lightly toss together in a 13-by-9-inch pan. Set aside.

5. **TO MAKE THE WHITE GELATIN:** In a medium bowl, dissolve the unflavored gelatin in the boiling water. Let cool slightly and then whisk in the sweetened condensed milk, until smooth. Let cool for 15 minutes.

6. When cooled, gently pour over the orange and blue gelatin cubes. Cover with plastic wrap and refrigerate overnight.

7. Cut into squares, to serve.

DAGOBAH SWAMP VINES

One bite of these crispy chocolate-butterscotch no-bake treats, and you'll fight off a vine snake for another.

DAGOBAH SWAMP VINES

Prep Time: 30 minutes
V* | **Yield:** 36 cookies
Difficulty: Easy

One 12-ounce bag semisweet chocolate chips
One 11-ounce bag butterscotch chips
6 ounces dark green candy melts
One 12-ounce bag crispy chow mein noodles
1 cup salted dry-roasted peanuts
One 3-ounce container tiny rainbow marshmallows

1. Line two large-rimmed baking sheets with waxed paper or parchment paper; set aside.

2. In a microwave-safe bowl combine the chocolate and butterscotch chips. Heat in 30-second increments until melted and smooth, stirring often. Set aside.

3. Place the green candy melts in a separate microwaveable bowl. Heat and melt just as you did the chips. Stir until smooth; set aside.

4. Place chow mein noodles in a large bowl. Moving quickly, pour the melted chocolate and butterscotch chip mixture over the noodles. Gently fold to thoroughly coat the noodles, trying not to break them. Gently fold in the peanuts and marshmallows—they should be completely coated.

5. Pour the green melted candy over the mixture and gently fold one or two times to create green streaks throughout mixture.

6. Drop mixture by tablespoons onto prepared baking sheets. Place in refrigerator for 10 to 15 minutes or until chocolate is set.

NOTE: This can be made vegetarian by using vegetarian candy melts and marshmallows.

WON-TAUN TUNDRA TREATS

No tauntaun—or any other tundra-dwelling creature, human or otherwise—will be able to resist these crispy pastry purses filled with chocolate-hazelnut spread and banana slices.

WON-TAUN TUNDRA TREATS

Prep Time: 30 minutes | **Cook Time:** 15 minutes
V | **Yield:** 16 wontons
Difficulty: Medium

2 tablespoons granulated sugar
2 teaspoons ground cinnamon
16 wonton wrappers
5 tablespoons chocolate-hazelnut spread
1 large ripe banana, sliced very thin
1 large egg beaten with 1 tablespoon water
¼ cup powdered sugar

1. Preheat oven to 375°F. Line a large-rimmed baking sheet with parchment paper. In a small bowl, stir together the sugar and cinnamon; set aside.

2. Separate 4 wonton wrappers and place on a clean work surface. Place a scant teaspoon of chocolate-hazelnut spread in the center of each wrapper and top with 2 slices of banana. Sprinkle with a good pinch of the sugar-cinnamon mixture.

3. Working with one wonton at a time, dip your finger into the egg mixture and run it along all four sides of the wrapper. Bring two diagonal corners up to meet together, then bring the remaining corners up to meet at the center. Pinch the seams to seal. Repeat this process for the remaining wontons.

4. Place the prepared wontons on the baking sheet. Brush the outside of each wonton with the egg wash. Bake for 13 to 15 minutes or until crisp and golden brown.

5. Let cool for 5 minutes on the baking sheet. With a fine sifter, dust the wontons with powdered sugar.

WOOKIEE-OOKIEES

No need to wait for the Wookiee holiday of Life Day to bake up these bite-size versions of everyone's favorite furry friends. These adorable treats will have you roaring with delight all year round!

WOOKIEE-OOKIEES

Prep Time: 1 hour 10 minutes | **Cook Time:** 10 minutes
V | **Yield:** About 12 cookies
Difficulty: Medium

3 cups all-purpose flour
1 teaspoon baking powder
1 teaspoon ground cinnamon
¼ teaspoon ground nutmeg
¼ teaspoon kosher salt
1 cup (2 sticks) unsalted butter, softened
½ cup packed light brown sugar
½ cup granulated sugar
1 large egg
2 tablespoons molasses
1 teaspoon vanilla extract
Black icing, for decorating
White icing, for decorating

1. In a medium bowl, whisk together the flour, baking powder, cinnamon, nutmeg, and salt. Set aside.

2. In the bowl of an electric mixer, cream the butter, brown sugar, and granulated sugar for about 5 to 6 minutes, until fluffy. Mix in the egg, molasses, and vanilla.

3. Add the flour mixture, mixing until the dough just comes together. Halve the dough and wrap each half in plastic wrap. Refrigerate for 1 hour.

4. Preheat the oven to 350°F. Prep two baking sheets with silicone baking mats or parchment paper.

5. Roll out the dough to a ¼-inch thickness. Use a gingerbread person–shape cutter to cut out shapes and transfer them to the prepped baking sheets. Use the back of a knife to create fur marks.

6. Bake for 10 minutes, then transfer the cookies to a wire rack to cool. Use the black and white icings to create face details. Let dry completely.

BESPIN CLOUD DROPS

These melt-in-your-mouth meringue drops resemble the colorful clouds of Tibanna gas that gently drift through the atmosphere around the planet Bespin. Whip up these dainty delights next time you see clouds in the forecast!

BESPIN CLOUD DROPS

Prep Time: 15 minutes | **Cook Time:** 1 hour 30 minutes
V, GF | **Yield:** Servings vary
Difficulty: Medium

3 egg whites
½ teaspoon cream of tartar
¾ cup granulated sugar
1 tablespoon desert pear syrup or grenadine
Light blue food coloring

1. Combine the egg whites and cream of tartar in a medium bowl and beat on medium speed using electric mixer until soft peaks form.
2. Turn the speed up to high and begin adding the sugar in a slow stream.

3. Beat until the sugar is completely dissolved, then quickly beat in the desert pear syrup or grenadine.

4. Preheat the oven to 200°F and line a baking sheet with parchment paper.

5. Drop dollops of the meringue onto the baking sheet using a spoon, then form into rough cloud shapes.

6. Dip a toothpick into the blue food coloring and swirl it through each cloud to add a little more color.

7. Bake for 1½ hours, then turn off the heat and prop the oven door open just a little. Let the meringues cool for another hour or so.

MUSTAFARIAN LAVA BUNS

The temperatures on the magma-covered world of Mustafar are as hot as an oven. This sweet red bread with a cracked, blackened exterior resembles the planet's scorching surface, making it the perfect treat for any hungry Dark Lord of the Sith.

MUSTAFARIAN LAVA BUNS

Prep Time: 2 hours | **Cook Time:** 20 minutes
V, GF* | Yield: 12 buns
Difficulty: Hard

BUNS:

1½ cups warm milk

1 tablespoon unsalted butter, melted

1 tablespoon granulated sugar

1 teaspoon kosher salt

2 teaspoons instant dry yeast

Red gel food coloring, as needed

3 cups all-purpose flour, plus more for dusting

TOPPING:

1 cup rice flour

1 teaspoon instant dry yeast

1 tablespoon granulated sugar

1 tablespoon vegetable oil

¾ cup warm water

Black gel food coloring, as needed

½ teaspoon coarse salt

1. **TO MAKE THE BUNS:** In a medium bowl, combine the milk, butter, sugar, salt, yeast, and enough food coloring to give you a nice robust red color. Gradually add the flour until you have a nice soft dough that isn't too sticky. Turn out onto a lightly floured surface and

knead for a couple of minutes, until it bounces back when poked. Place in a clean bowl and cover with plastic. Set in a warm place to rise for about 1 hour, or until doubled in size.

2. Line a baking sheet with parchment paper or a silicone mat. Turn the dough out of the bowl and divide into 12 equal portions. Loosely roll each of these into a smooth ball and set on the prepared baking sheet. Cover and let the dough begin to rise again while you make the topping.

3. **TO MAKE THE TOPPING:** Whisk together all the ingredients in a small bowl until smooth. Set aside and let rise, along with the rolls, for about 20 minutes. Then, using a pastry brush, brush a thick layer of the topping onto each roll, covering as much as possible. Preheat the oven to 400°F and let the rolls rise another 20 minutes.

4. When ready, bake the rolls for 15 to 20 minutes, until puffed and firm to the touch. Let cool for about 10 minutes before serving.

NOTE: This can be made gluten free by using a gluten-free instant dry yeast.

BB-8 CUPCAKES

In the words of Leia Organa, "never underestimate a droid"—or these treats, which will surely appeal to all ages and tastes!

BB-8 CUPCAKES

Prep Time: 2 hours 30 minutes | **Cook Time:** 15 minutes
V | **Yield:** 12 cupcakes
Difficulty: Medium

1½ cups all-purpose flour
⅔ cup granulated sugar
2 teaspoons baking powder
⅔ cup whole milk
¼ cup unsalted butter, very soft
1 large egg
1 teaspoon vanilla extract
One 16-ounce can vanilla frosting, divided
12 plain donut holes
Orange and black gel food coloring
Black or brown mini and regular-size round candy-coated chocolate pieces
Silver dragees

1. Preheat oven to 350°F. Line a cupcake pan with 12 paper or foil liners. In a medium mixing bowl combine flour, sugar, and baking powder. Add milk, butter, egg,

and vanilla. Beat with a hand mixer on low speed until combined. Beat on medium speed for 1 minute. Divide batter among cupcake liners in pan (two-thirds full to ensure rounded tops after baking). Bake about 15 minutes or until a toothpick inserted comes out clean. Cool on a wire rack.

2. Place about 1 cup of canned frosting in a small microwave-safe bowl. Microwave on high for 15 seconds, then stir. Continue to microwave and stir, 10 seconds at a time, until frosting is just soft enough to pour from a spoon. Dip tops of cupcakes into the soft frosting and return to cooling rack. With a sharp knife, remove a ¼-inch slice from bottom of each donut hole. If necessary, reheat frosting to keep it spoonable. With a fork, hold a donut hole over bowl of softened frosting. Spoon frosting over donut hole to cover. Carefully place the frosted donut hole on top of a frosted cupcake. Chill cupcakes a few minutes to set frosting.

3. Divide remaining unmelted frosting between two small bowls. Tint one portion orange and the other portion gray. Place colored frosting in disposable decorating bags. Snip tips of bags to make very small openings. Decorate cupcakes with colored frosting, making stripes, circles, and dots. Add candy-coated chocolate pieces and silver dragees.

KYBER SCONES

These simple scones have a sugary coating that shimmers like kyber crystals—the mysterious gems found at the heart of lightsabers. There's no denying that the Force is strong with this snack!

KYBER SCONES

Prep Time: 15 minutes | **Cook Time:** 15 minutes
V | **Yield:** 8 large scones
Difficulty: Medium

SCONES:
2 cups all-purpose flour
⅓ cup granulated sugar
1½ teaspoons baking powder
¼ teaspoon kosher salt
½ cup (1 stick) cold unsalted butter, cubed
¼ cup softened cream cheese
1 large egg
½ cup buttermilk
1 tablespoon lemon juice
1 teaspoon vanilla extract

GLAZE:
¾ cup confectioners' sugar
1½ tablespoons whole milk
½ teaspoon almond extract
½ teaspoon vanilla extract
Decorative blue sugar sprinkles

1. Preheat oven to 400°F. Prep a baking sheet with parchment greased with nonstick spray.
2. **TO MAKE THE SCONES:** In a large bowl whisk together flour, sugar, baking powder, and salt.
3. Mix in the butter and cream cheese, until crumbly.
4. Add the egg, buttermilk, lemon juice, and vanilla, until just combined.
5. Scoop rounds of dough 2 inches apart onto the prepped baking sheets.
6. Bake for 16 to 18 minutes. Transfer to a wire rack and let cool.
7. **TO MAKE THE GLAZE:** In a small bowl, whisk together the confectioners' sugar, milk, almond extract, and vanilla. Drizzle over scones. Sprinkle with blue sugar sprinkles, to serve.

KLATOOINE CRÊPES

Hutts will eat just about anything that you put in front of them. These coconut-filled crêpes capture the color and texture of their favorite snack, the Klatooine paddy frog, in the form of a delicious frog-free dessert!

KLATOOINE CRÊPES

Prep Time: 1 hour 20 minutes | **Cook Time:** 25 minutes
V | **Yield:** 8 crêpes
Difficulty: Hard

FILLING:
½ cup unsweetened shredded coconut
½ cup packed light brown sugar
¼ cup full-fat coconut milk

CRÊPES:
1 cup full-fat coconut milk
1 teaspoon pandan extract
2 large eggs
2 tablespoons unsalted butter, melted
1 cup all-purpose flour
½ teaspoon kosher salt

1. **TO MAKE THE FILLING:** In a medium saucepan over medium-low heat, stir together the coconut, brown sugar, and coconut milk, and cook for 10 to 15 minutes, until the ingredients are combined and slightly dry. Set aside to cool.

2. **TO MAKE THE CRÊPES:** Combine the coconut milk, pandan extract, eggs, butter, flour, and salt in a blender. Blend until just combined. Chill in the refrigerator for 1 hour.

3. Heat a medium nonstick skillet over medium heat. Add ¼ cup of crêpe batter, swirling until the batter coats the bottom of the skillet. Cook for 30 seconds, or until the edges are dry and the center is just set. Flip over and cook for another 15 seconds. Remove and set aside. Repeat with the rest of the crêpe batter.

4. Add 1 tablespoon of filling along the center of a crêpe. Fold the bottom over, then the sides, and finally the top. Serve seam-side down. Repeat with the rest of the crêpes and the filling.

TIE FIGHTER ICE CREAM SANDWICHES

The scream of an approaching fleet of TIE fighters may have struck fear in the hearts of any enemy of the Empire, but you'll only make friends when you build a batch of these frozen treats.

TIE FIGHTER ICE CREAM SANDWICHES

Prep Time: 4 to 24 hours | **Cook Time:** 10 minutes
V | **Yield:** 10 ice cream sandwiches
Difficulty: Hard

¼ cup unsalted butter, softened
½ cup chocolate-hazelnut spread
1 cup granulated sugar
½ teaspoon baking powder
1 large egg
¼ cup whole milk
1 teaspoon vanilla extract
2¾ cups all-purpose flour, plus more for dusting
½ cup semisweet chocolate chips
1 teaspoon shortening
1 quart desired ice cream (chocolate, mint chip, or chocolate chip)

1. In a large mixing bowl, beat butter and chocolate-hazelnut spread with a hand mixer on medium to high speed for 30 seconds or until softened. Add sugar and baking powder. Beat until combined, scraping sides of bowl occasionally. Beat in egg, milk, and vanilla until combined. Beat in as much flour as you can with the mixer. Stir in remaining flour with a wooden spoon.

2. Shape dough into a disk. Wrap dough in plastic wrap and chill for 4 to 24 hours.

3. Preheat oven to 375°F. Line two rimmed baking sheets with parchment paper. On a lightly floured surface, roll out chilled dough to 20-by-12-inch rectangle (¼-inch thickness). Using a knife (or pizza cutter), cut dough into 20 wings. Transfer wings with a spatula to prepared baking sheets. Prick each cookie several times with a fork. Bake for 8 to 10 minutes or until cookies are firm in center. Let cool on the pan for 5 minutes. Transfer to a wire rack to cool completely.

4. Place chocolate chips and shortening in a small microwave-safe bowl. Microwave on high for 45 seconds, then stir. Microwave for 30 seconds more or until chocolate is melted, stirring every 30 seconds.

5. Place melted chocolate in a decorating bag. Snip tip of bag to make a tiny opening. Decorate tops of cookies with piped chocolate to resemble a TIE fighter wing. Chill cookies until ready to fill with ice cream, at least 30 minutes.

6. Place a small, round scoop (¼ cup) of ice cream between 2 chilled cookies and very gently press together to avoid breaking the cookies. (The ice cream should stay just in middle of the sandwich.) Store in freezer.

PASAANA POPS

When Rey embarks on a quest to find Emperor Palpatine, she finds herself on the planet of Pasaana. The desert planet is home to the Festival of the Ancestors, a colorful celebration full of dancing and merriment that takes place once every forty-two years. With this sweet homage to the bright colors of Pasaana, you'll learn how to decorate delicious snacks with breakfast cereal.

PASAANA POPS

Prep Time: 3 hours
V, GF* | Yield: 6 pops
Difficulty: Easy

3 large bananas, halved crosswise
1½ cups strawberry yogurt
2 cups fruit cereal

SPECIAL TOOLS:
6 popsicle sticks

1. Place the popsicle sticks into the bananas.
2. Dip into the yogurt, then roll into the cereal. Place on a parchment-lined plate and freeze for 2 to 3 hours.
3. Let soften slightly for 2 to 3 minutes before serving.

> **NOTE:** Use a gluten-free fruit cereal to make this gluten free.

FIND MORE RECIPES FROM STAR WARS

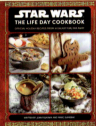

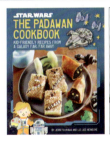

INSIGHT EDITIONS

PO Box 3088
San Rafael, CA 94912
www.insighteditions.com

Find us on Facebook:
www.facebook.com/InsightEditions
Follow us on Instagram:
@insighteditions

© & ™ 2025 LUCASFILM LTD. Used Under Authorization.

All rights reserved. This revised edition published by Insight Editions, San Rafael, California, in 2025.

No part of this book may be reproduced in any form without written permission from the publisher.

ISBN: 979-8-88663-898-1

Publisher: Raoul Goff
SVP, Group Publisher: Vanessa Lopez
VP, Creative: Chrissy Kwasnik
VP, Manufacturing: Alix Nicholaeff
Editorial Director: Thom O'Hearn
Art Director: Stuart Smith
Designer: Brooke McCullum
Associate Editor: Sami Alvarado
VP, Senior Executive Project Editor: Vicki Jaeger
Managing Editor: Shannon Ballesteros
Production Manager: Deena Hashem
Strategic Production Planner: Lina s Palma-Temena

ROOTS of PEACE   REPLANTED PAPER

Insight Editions, in association with Roots of Peace, will plant two trees for each tree used in the manufacturing of this product.

Manufactured in China by Insight Editions

10 9 8 7 6 5 4 3 2 1

RECIPE SOURCES

Pages 29, 36, 45, 85, 89 .... previously published in *Star Wars: Galaxy's Edge* by Chelsea Monroe-Cassel and Marc Sumerak in 2019.

Pages 57, 73, 77, 93, 105 .... previously published in *Star Wars: Galactic Baking* in 2021.

Pages 53, 81, 101 .... previously published in *Star Wars: The Life Day Cookbook* by Jenn Fujikawa and Marc Sumerak in 2021.

Pages 9, 13, 17, 33, 41, 61, 65, 69, 109 .... previously published in *Star Wars: The Padawan Cookbook* by Jenn Fujikawa and Liz Lee Heinecke in 2022.

Pages 21, 25, 49, 97 .... previously published in *Star Wars: The Ultimate Cookbook* by Jenn Fujikawa and Marc Sumerak in 2023.